Success With Math Tests

New York • Toronto • London • Auckland • Sydney
Mexico City • New Delhi • Hong Kong • Buenos Aires

Teaching *Resources*

State Standards Correlations

To find out how this book helps you meet your state's standards, log on to **www.scholastic.com/ssw**

Cover design by Ka-Yeon Kim-Li
Interior illustrations by Kate Flanagan
Interior design by Creative Pages Inc.

ISBN-13 978-0-545-20066-0
ISBN-10 0-545-20066-0

Contents

Introduction

In this book, you will find eight Practice Tests designed to help students prepare to take standardized tests. Each test has 20–30 multiple-choice items that closely resemble the kinds of questions students will have to answer on "real" tests. Each part of the test will take 30–40 minutes for students to complete.

The Math skills measured in these tests and the types of questions are based on detailed analyses and correlations of the five most widely used standardized tests and the curriculum standards measured by many statewide tests, including the following:

Stanford Achievement Test   California's STAR Test
CTBS TerraNova   TAAS (Texas)
Metropolitan Achievement Test   MCAS (Massachusetts)
Iowa Test of Basic Skills   FCAT (Florida)
California Achievement Test   New York

How to Use the Tests

Tell students how much time they will have to complete the test. Encourage students to work quickly and carefully and to keep track of the remaining time—just as they would in a real testing session. You may have students mark their answers directly on the test pages, or you may have them use a copy of the **Answer Sheet**. An answer sheet appears at the end of each test. The answer sheet will help students become accustomed to filling in bubbles on a real test. It may also make the tests easier for you to score.

We do not recommend the use of calculators. For Practice Tests 2 and 6, students will need an inch ruler and a centimeter ruler to answer some of the questions.

At the back of this book, you will find **Tested Skills** charts and **Answer Keys** for the eight Practice Tests. The Tested Skills charts list the skills measured in each test and the test questions that measure each skill. These charts may be helpful to you in determining what kinds of questions students answered incorrectly, what skills they may be having trouble with, and who may need further instruction in particular skills. To score a Practice Test, refer to the Answer Key for that test. The Answer Key lists the correct response to each question.

To score a Practice Test, go through the test and mark each question answered correctly. Add the total number of questions answered correctly to find the student's test score. To find a percentage score, divide the number answered correctly by the total number of questions. For example, the percentage score for a student who answers 20 out of 25 questions correctly is $20 \div 25 = 0.80$, or 80%. You might want to have students correct their own tests. This will give them a chance to see where they made mistakes and what they need to do to improve their scores on the next test.

On the next page of this book, you will find **Test-Taking Tips**. You may want to share these tips and strategies with students before they begin working on the Practice Tests.

Test-Taking Tips: Mathematics

1. For each part of the test, read the directions carefully so you know what to do. Then read the directions again—just to make sure.

2. Look for key words and phrases to help you decide what each question is asking and what kind of computation you need to do. Examples of key words: *less than, greatest, least, farther, longest, divided equally.*

3. To help solve a problem, write a number sentence or equation.

4. Use scrap paper (or extra space on the test page) to write down the numbers and information you need to solve a problem.

5. If a question has a picture or diagram, study it carefully. Draw your own picture or diagram if it will help you solve a problem.

6. Try to solve each problem before you look at the answer choices. (In some tests, the correct answer may be "Not Given" or "Not Here," so you will want to be sure of your answer. In these Practice Tests, some of the Math questions use "NG" for "Not Given.")

7. Check your work carefully before you finish. (In many questions, you can check your answer by working backwards to see if the numbers work out correctly.)

8. If you are not sure which answer is correct, cross out every answer that you know is wrong. Then make your best guess.

9. To complete a number sentence or equation, try all the answer choices until you find the one that works.

10. When working with fractions, always reduce (or rename) the fractions to their lowest parts. When working with decimals, keep the decimal points lined up correctly.

Practice
Test 1

Numeration and
Number Concepts

Practice Test 1

Directions. Choose the best answer to each question. Mark your answer.

1. Becky was counting the children in a line.

2, 4, 6, 8, __10__

Which number should come next?
- (A) 9
- (B) 10
- (C) 11
- (D) 12

2. There are 10 pencils in each bundle.

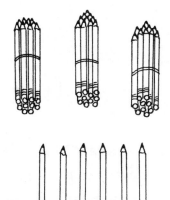

How many pencils are there in all?
- (F) 9
- (G) 30
- (H) 35
- (J) 36

3. The Nile River is four thousand one hundred sixty miles long. Which number means four thousand one hundred sixty?
- (A) 40,160
- (B) 4106
- (C) 4016
- (D) 4160

4. Great Bear Lake is 1463 feet deep. What is that number in words?
- (F) one hundred four sixty-three
- (G) one thousand forty-six three
- (H) one thousand four hundred sixty-three
- (J) ten thousand four hundred sixty-three

5. Which teacher has an odd number of students in his or her class?

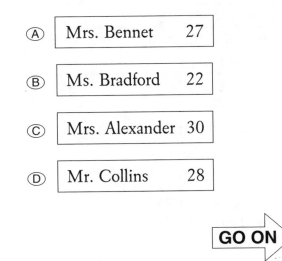

- (A) Mrs. Bennet 27
- (B) Ms. Bradford 22
- (C) Mrs. Alexander 30
- (D) Mr. Collins 28

GO ON

Scholastic Inc.

Practice Test 1 *(continued)*

6. The chart shows the number of people who live in each town.

Town	Number of People
Ascot	804
Grant	791
Stoneham	845
Wardsboro	973

Which town has the least number of people?

- Ⓕ Ascot
- Ⓖ Grant
- Ⓗ Stoneham
- Ⓙ Wardsboro

7. The chart shows the height of four buildings in Denver, Colorado.

Building	Height (feet)
MCI Tower	522
Amoco Building	448
Qwest Tower	507
1999 Broadway	544

Which building is tallest?

- Ⓐ MCI Tower
- Ⓑ Amoco Building
- Ⓒ Qwest Tower
- Ⓓ 1999 Broadway

8. Which number means
5000 + 60 + 8?

- Ⓕ 568
- Ⓖ 5068
- Ⓗ 5608
- Ⓙ 50,608

9. There are about 1850 kinds of beetles in the world. What does the 8 stand for in 1850?

- Ⓐ 8 thousands
- Ⓑ 8 hundreds
- Ⓒ 8 tens
- Ⓓ 8 ones

10. Mr. Evans drove 3295 miles last month. What is that number rounded to the nearest hundred?

- Ⓕ 3000
- Ⓖ 3200
- Ⓗ 3300
- Ⓙ 4000

GO ON

Scholastic Inc.

Practice Test 1 *(continued)*

11. Wanda is making a bead necklace with this pattern.

If this pattern continues, what will the next two beads look like?

Ⓐ

Ⓑ

Ⓒ

Ⓓ

12. Mr. Craig wrote this number pattern on the blackboard.

3, 7, 11, 15, _____

If the same pattern continues, what should the next number be?

Ⓕ 16
Ⓖ 18
Ⓗ 19
Ⓙ 20

13. Which street has an even number?

Ⓐ | 27 Street |

Ⓑ | 39 Street |

Ⓒ | 15 Street |

Ⓓ | 48 Street |

14. Which number is marked on the number line?

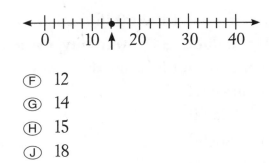

Ⓕ 12
Ⓖ 14
Ⓗ 15
Ⓙ 18

15. On Monday, 715 people went to the mall. On Tuesday, 892 people went to the mall. **About** how many people went to the mall in those two days?

Ⓐ 1200
Ⓑ 1400
Ⓒ 1600
Ⓓ 1800

GO ON

Practice Test 1 *(continued)*

16. What number is shown on the number line?

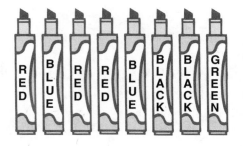

- (F) 203
- (G) 213
- (H) 230
- (J) 240

17. Jeremy had $104.00 in the bank. He took out $47.00 to buy a video game. <u>About</u> how much money did he have left?

- (A) $25.00
- (B) $50.00
- (C) $80.00
- (D) $100.00

18. Which is another way to write $4 + 4 + 4 + 4 + 4$?

- (F) $4 + 5$
- (G) $4 \times 4 \times 4 \times 4 \times 4$
- (H) $20 + 4$
- (J) 4×5

19. Willy has 8 markers of different colors.

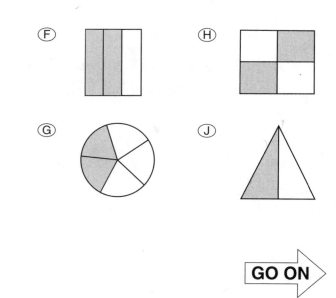

What fractional part of the markers are red?

- (A) $\frac{1}{4}$
- (B) $\frac{3}{5}$
- (C) $\frac{1}{2}$
- (D) $\frac{3}{8}$

20. Which figure shows $\frac{2}{3}$ shaded?

(F)　(H)

(G)　(J)

GO ON

Practice Test 1 *(continued)*

21. Which number goes in the box to make this number sentence true?

$15 \times 1 = \square$

- (A) 0
- (B) 1
- (C) 15
- (D) 16

22. Which number sentence goes with this fact?

$8 + 6 = 14$

- (F) $8 - 6 = 2$
- (G) $14 - 6 = 8$
- (H) $8 \times 6 = 48$
- (J) $14 + 6 = 20$

23. Which number sentence is true?
- (A) $7 \times 0 = 0$
- (B) $7 - 0 = 0$
- (C) $7 \times 1 = 1$
- (D) $7 + 0 = 1 + 7$

24. Which box of cereal weighs most?

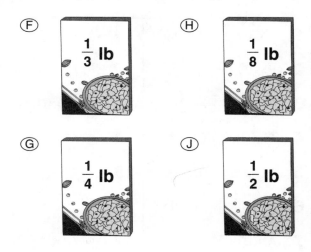

25. The chart shows how far four children hiked on a trail.

Polly	$\frac{3}{4}$ mile
Mark	$\frac{2}{5}$ mile
Stu	$\frac{1}{2}$ mile
John	$\frac{2}{3}$ mile

Which lists the four children in order from the shortest hike to the longest?
- (A) Polly, Mark, Stu, John
- (B) Mark, Stu, John, Polly
- (C) Stu, Mark, Polly, John
- (D) John, Polly, Mark, Stu

ANSWER SHEET

Practice Test # 1

Student Name _____ Grade _____

Teacher Name _____ Date _____

MATHEMATICS

1 Ⓐ Ⓑ Ⓒ Ⓓ Ⓔ	11 Ⓐ Ⓑ Ⓒ Ⓓ Ⓔ	21 Ⓐ Ⓑ Ⓒ Ⓓ Ⓔ	31 Ⓐ Ⓑ Ⓒ Ⓓ Ⓔ
2 Ⓕ Ⓖ Ⓗ Ⓙ Ⓚ	12 Ⓕ Ⓖ Ⓗ Ⓙ Ⓚ	22 Ⓕ Ⓖ Ⓗ Ⓙ Ⓚ	32 Ⓕ Ⓖ Ⓗ Ⓙ Ⓚ
3 Ⓐ Ⓑ Ⓒ Ⓓ Ⓔ	13 Ⓐ Ⓑ Ⓒ Ⓓ Ⓔ	23 Ⓐ Ⓑ Ⓒ Ⓓ Ⓔ	33 Ⓐ Ⓑ Ⓒ Ⓓ Ⓔ
4 Ⓕ Ⓖ Ⓗ Ⓙ Ⓚ	14 Ⓕ Ⓖ Ⓗ Ⓙ Ⓚ	24 Ⓕ Ⓖ Ⓗ Ⓙ Ⓚ	34 Ⓕ Ⓖ Ⓗ Ⓙ Ⓚ
5 Ⓐ Ⓑ Ⓒ Ⓓ Ⓔ	15 Ⓐ Ⓑ Ⓒ Ⓓ Ⓔ	25 Ⓐ Ⓑ Ⓒ Ⓓ Ⓔ	35 Ⓐ Ⓑ Ⓒ Ⓓ Ⓔ
6 Ⓕ Ⓖ Ⓗ Ⓙ Ⓚ	16 Ⓕ Ⓖ Ⓗ Ⓙ Ⓚ	26 Ⓕ Ⓖ Ⓗ Ⓙ Ⓚ	36 Ⓕ Ⓖ Ⓗ Ⓙ Ⓚ
7 Ⓐ Ⓑ Ⓒ Ⓓ Ⓔ	17 Ⓐ Ⓑ Ⓒ Ⓓ Ⓔ	27 Ⓐ Ⓑ Ⓒ Ⓓ Ⓔ	37 Ⓐ Ⓑ Ⓒ Ⓓ Ⓔ
8 Ⓕ Ⓖ Ⓗ Ⓙ Ⓚ	18 Ⓕ Ⓖ Ⓗ Ⓙ Ⓚ	28 Ⓕ Ⓖ Ⓗ Ⓙ Ⓚ	38 Ⓕ Ⓖ Ⓗ Ⓙ Ⓚ
9 Ⓐ Ⓑ Ⓒ Ⓓ Ⓔ	19 Ⓐ Ⓑ Ⓒ Ⓓ Ⓔ	29 Ⓐ Ⓑ Ⓒ Ⓓ Ⓔ	39 Ⓐ Ⓑ Ⓒ Ⓓ Ⓔ
10 Ⓕ Ⓖ Ⓗ Ⓙ Ⓚ	20 Ⓕ Ⓖ Ⓗ Ⓙ Ⓚ	30 Ⓕ Ⓖ Ⓗ Ⓙ Ⓚ	40 Ⓕ Ⓖ Ⓗ Ⓙ Ⓚ

Practice
Test 2

Geometry and
Measurement

Practice Test 2

Directions. Choose the best answer to each question. Mark your answer.

1. Which unit should be used to measure how tall you are?

ⓐ gallons

ⓑ pounds

ⓒ inches

ⓓ yards

2. Marina started doing her homework at 3:15 P.M. She finished 40 minutes later. Which clock shows the time she finished?

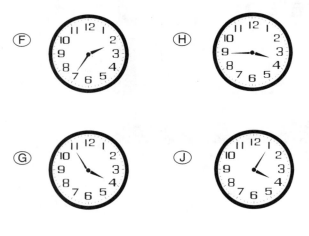

3. Kent had these coins in his pocket. What is the total value of the coins?

ⓐ 61¢   ⓒ 52¢

ⓑ 56¢   ⓓ 51¢

This graph shows the amount of snow that fell each month in the winter of 2000–2001. Use the graph to answer questions 4 and 5.

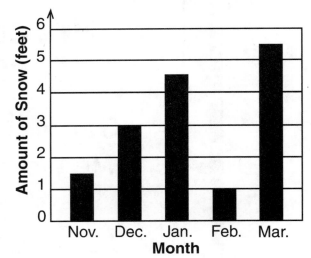

4. In which month did the greatest amount of snow fall?

ⓕ November

ⓖ January

ⓗ February

ⓙ March

5. How much snow fell in December?

ⓐ $4\frac{1}{2}$ ft

ⓑ 3 ft

ⓒ $1\frac{1}{2}$ ft

ⓓ 1 f

GO ON

Practice Test 2 *(continued)*

6. Which part of the house has the shape of a triangle?

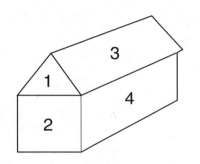

   Ⓕ part 1
   Ⓖ part 2
   Ⓗ part 3
   Ⓙ part 4

7. Which shape has 6 faces?

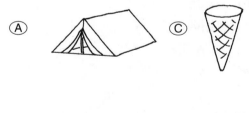

8. Which figure has only two sides of equal length?

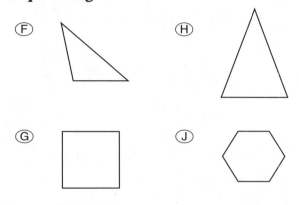

9. Look at Figure A.

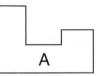

Which piece of the puzzle has the same size and shape?

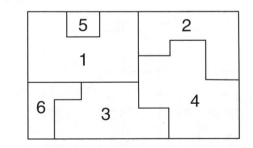

   Ⓐ piece 1
   Ⓑ piece 2
   Ⓒ piece 3
   Ⓓ piece 4

Practice Test 2 *(continued)*

10. Each card will be folded in half on the dotted line. On which card will the two halves match exactly?

Ⓕ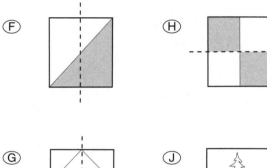

Ⓗ

Ⓖ

Ⓙ

11. What is the area of this figure (in square units)?

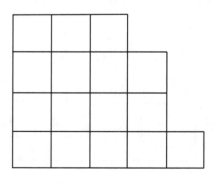

Ⓐ 16
Ⓑ 15
Ⓒ 14
Ⓓ 12

12. Matt found this money on the table.

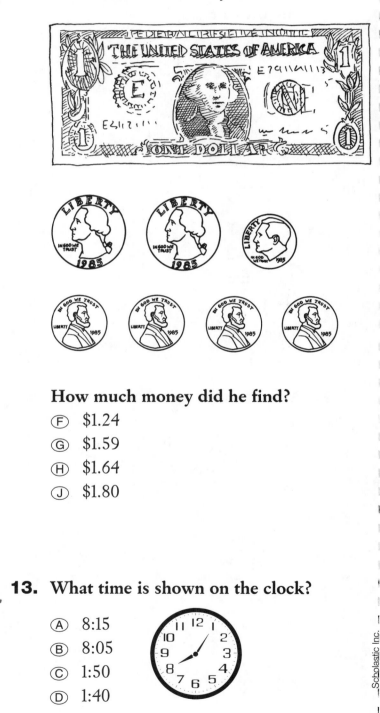

How much money did he find?

Ⓕ $1.24
Ⓖ $1.59
Ⓗ $1.64
Ⓙ $1.80

13. What time is shown on the clock?

Ⓐ 8:15
Ⓑ 8:05
Ⓒ 1:50
Ⓓ 1:40

GO ON

Scholastic Inc.

Practice Test 2 *(continued)*

14. A boy in third grade is most likely to weigh about —

    Ⓕ 100 pounds

    Ⓖ 60 pounds

    Ⓗ 40 pounds

    Ⓙ 20 pounds

15. If you fill a large cooking pot with water, about how much water will it hold?

    Ⓐ 2 gallons

    Ⓑ 20 gallons

    Ⓒ 200 gallons

    Ⓓ 2000 gallons

16. Which unit should be used to measure how far a school bus travels each day?

    Ⓕ pounds

    Ⓖ feet

    Ⓗ gallons

    Ⓙ miles

17. How long is the roll of mints? (Use your inch ruler.)

    Ⓐ 2 inches

    Ⓑ 3 inches

    Ⓒ 4 inches

    Ⓓ 5 inches

18. How long is the grasshopper? (Use your centimeter ruler.)

    Ⓕ 4 centimeters

    Ⓖ 5 centimeters

    Ⓗ 6 centimeters

    Ⓙ 7 centimeters

Practice Test 2 *(continued)*

19. This box will be turned on its side in the direction of the arrow.

Which picture shows the box after it has been turned?

Ⓐ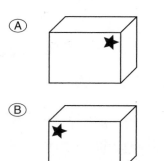

Ⓒ

Ⓑ

Ⓓ

20. Where is the 🌲 located on the grid?

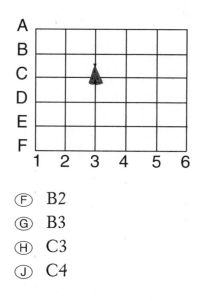

Ⓕ B2
Ⓖ B3
Ⓗ C3
Ⓙ C4

This graph shows how many sandwiches children ate at the school picnic. Use the graph to answer questions 21 and 22.

Sandwiches Eaten

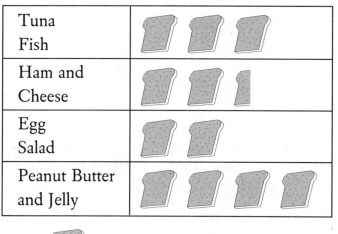

🍞 = 5 sandwiches

21. How many tuna fish sandwiches did children eat?

Ⓐ 3
Ⓑ 10
Ⓒ 15
Ⓓ 20

22. Which kind of sandwich was eaten most?

Ⓕ tuna fish
Ⓖ ham and cheese
Ⓗ egg salad
Ⓙ peanut butter and jelly

Scholastic Inc.

ANSWER SHEET

Student Name _____ Grade _____

Teacher Name _____ Date _____

MATHEMATICS

1 Ⓐ Ⓑ Ⓒ Ⓓ Ⓔ   11 Ⓐ Ⓑ Ⓒ Ⓓ Ⓔ   21 Ⓐ Ⓑ Ⓒ Ⓓ Ⓔ   31 Ⓐ Ⓑ Ⓒ Ⓓ Ⓔ

2 Ⓕ Ⓖ Ⓗ Ⓙ Ⓚ   12 Ⓕ Ⓖ Ⓗ Ⓙ Ⓚ   22 Ⓕ Ⓖ Ⓗ Ⓙ Ⓚ   32 Ⓕ Ⓖ Ⓗ Ⓙ Ⓚ

3 Ⓐ Ⓑ Ⓒ Ⓓ Ⓔ   13 Ⓐ Ⓑ Ⓒ Ⓓ Ⓔ   23 Ⓐ Ⓑ Ⓒ Ⓓ Ⓔ   33 Ⓐ Ⓑ Ⓒ Ⓓ Ⓔ

4 Ⓕ Ⓖ Ⓗ Ⓙ Ⓚ   14 Ⓕ Ⓖ Ⓗ Ⓙ Ⓚ   24 Ⓕ Ⓖ Ⓗ Ⓙ Ⓚ   34 Ⓕ Ⓖ Ⓗ Ⓙ Ⓚ

5 Ⓐ Ⓑ Ⓒ Ⓓ Ⓔ   15 Ⓐ Ⓑ Ⓒ Ⓓ Ⓔ   25 Ⓐ Ⓑ Ⓒ Ⓓ Ⓔ   35 Ⓐ Ⓑ Ⓒ Ⓓ Ⓔ

6 Ⓕ Ⓖ Ⓗ Ⓙ Ⓚ   16 Ⓕ Ⓖ Ⓗ Ⓙ Ⓚ   26 Ⓕ Ⓖ Ⓗ Ⓙ Ⓚ   36 Ⓕ Ⓖ Ⓗ Ⓙ Ⓚ

7 Ⓐ Ⓑ Ⓒ Ⓓ Ⓔ   17 Ⓐ Ⓑ Ⓒ Ⓓ Ⓔ   27 Ⓐ Ⓑ Ⓒ Ⓓ Ⓔ   37 Ⓐ Ⓑ Ⓒ Ⓓ Ⓔ

8 Ⓕ Ⓖ Ⓗ Ⓙ Ⓚ   18 Ⓕ Ⓖ Ⓗ Ⓙ Ⓚ   28 Ⓕ Ⓖ Ⓗ Ⓙ Ⓚ   38 Ⓕ Ⓖ Ⓗ Ⓙ Ⓚ

9 Ⓐ Ⓑ Ⓒ Ⓓ Ⓔ   19 Ⓐ Ⓑ Ⓒ Ⓓ Ⓔ   29 Ⓐ Ⓑ Ⓒ Ⓓ Ⓔ   39 Ⓐ Ⓑ Ⓒ Ⓓ Ⓔ

10 Ⓕ Ⓖ Ⓗ Ⓙ Ⓚ   20 Ⓕ Ⓖ Ⓗ Ⓙ Ⓚ   30 Ⓕ Ⓖ Ⓗ Ⓙ Ⓚ   40 Ⓕ Ⓖ Ⓗ Ⓙ Ⓚ

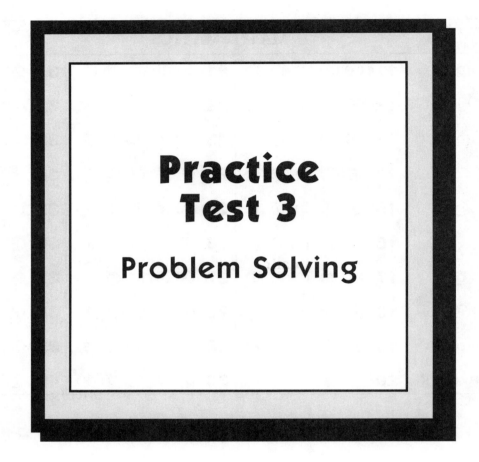

Practice
Test 3

Problem Solving

Practice Test 3

Directions. Choose the best answer to each question. Mark your answer. If the correct answer is *not given,* choose "NG."

1. Mr. Cole picked 125 apples and 68 pears from the trees in his yard.

125   68

How many fruits did he pick in all?

- Ⓐ 203
- Ⓑ 193
- Ⓒ 183
- Ⓓ 57
- Ⓔ NG

2. On Saturday, there were 52 boys and 39 girls at the playground. All together, how many children were at the playground on Saturday?

- Ⓕ 81
- Ⓖ 87
- Ⓗ 90
- Ⓙ 91
- Ⓚ NG

3. Carol saw these animals when she went on a nature walk.

Squirrels	8
Chipmunks	6
Birds	17

How many animals did she see in all?

- Ⓐ 31
- Ⓑ 30
- Ⓒ 23
- Ⓓ 14
- Ⓔ NG

4. Eliza had 320 ears of corn to sell at her farm stand. By the end of the day, she had sold 275 ears. How many ears of corn were left?

- Ⓕ 595
- Ⓖ 155
- Ⓗ 45
- Ⓙ 35
- Ⓚ NG

5. Mr. Wagner plans to drive 640 miles to Los Angeles. He has gone 492 miles so far. How many more miles does he have to go?

- Ⓐ 252
- Ⓑ 248
- Ⓒ 158
- Ⓓ 152
- Ⓔ NG

GO ON

Practice Test 3 *(continued)*

6. Henry practices playing the piano for 15 minutes each day. How much time does he spend practicing in 5 days?

Ⓕ 20 minutes

Ⓖ 55 minutes

Ⓗ 75 minutes

Ⓙ 90 minutes

Ⓚ NG

7. In Sue's classroom, there are 4 rows of desks and 9 desks in each row. How many desks are there in all?

Ⓐ 45

Ⓑ 36

Ⓒ 27

Ⓓ 13

Ⓔ NG

8. Five friends will share a bag of peanuts equally. There are 30 peanuts in the bag. How many peanuts will each person get?

Ⓕ 6

Ⓖ 7

Ⓗ 8

Ⓙ 9

Ⓚ NG

9. Kelly bought a gallon of milk for $3.94. She paid for it with a $5-dollar bill.

$3.94

How much change should she get?

Ⓐ $0.06

Ⓑ $0.60

Ⓒ $0.96

Ⓓ $1.06

Ⓔ NG

10. Mike bought a set of markers for $2.85. The tax was $0.16.

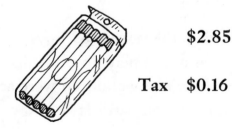

$2.85

Tax $0.16

What was the total cost of the markers?

Ⓕ $2.01

Ⓖ $2.68

Ⓗ $2.91

Ⓙ $3.05

Ⓚ NG

GO ON

Scholastic Inc.

Practice Test 3 *(continued)*

11. Abby's soccer game started at the time shown.

The game ended 1 hour 15 minutes later. What time did the game end?

Ⓐ 4:30
Ⓑ 4:45
Ⓒ 5:00
Ⓓ 5:15
Ⓔ NG

12. Mrs. Casey rides an exercise bike for 45 minutes each day.

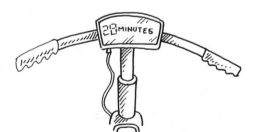

She has been riding for 28 minutes so far. How much longer does she have to ride?

Ⓕ 7 minutes
Ⓖ 13 minutes
Ⓗ 27 minutes
Ⓙ 73 minutes
Ⓚ NG

13. Cal bought these things at the store.

$2.05 $1.98 $1.10

<u>About</u> how much money did he spend in all?

Ⓐ $2
Ⓑ $5
Ⓒ $8
Ⓓ $10

14. Jamie went to a fair and bought a book of 50 tickets. Each ride takes 4 or 5 tickets. <u>About</u> how many rides can he take?

Ⓕ 5
Ⓖ 10
Ⓗ 20
Ⓙ 40

15. Kim wants to buy a video game player that costs $198. She has saved $47 so far. <u>About</u> how much more money does she need?

Ⓐ $50
Ⓑ $100
Ⓒ $150
Ⓓ $200

GO ON ⇨

Practice Test 3 *(continued)*

16. Jim is playing a game with this spinner.

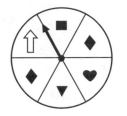

If he spins the spinner 10 times, what will he spin most often?

Ⓕ ◆

Ⓖ ♥

Ⓗ ■

Ⓙ ⇧

Ⓚ NG

17. Pia has these colored blocks in a box.

Color	Number of Blocks
Red	9
Yellow	8
Blue	4
Green	6
Orange	12

If Pia takes one block out of the box without looking, she is most likely to get what color?

Ⓐ red

Ⓑ yellow

Ⓒ green

Ⓓ orange

Ⓔ NG

18. Jo read 3 books last week. Dale read 1 more than Jo. Sam read twice as many books as Dale. How many books did Sam read?

Ⓕ 3

Ⓖ 4

Ⓗ 6

Ⓙ 8

Ⓚ NG

19. Tammy had 43 picture books. She gave 16 books to her little brother. Which number sentence should be used to find how many books she has left?

Ⓐ $43 - 16 = \square$

Ⓑ $43 + 16 = \square$

Ⓒ $16 - 43 = \square$

Ⓓ $43 \times 16 = \square$

Ⓔ NG

20. Mr. Lane bought 6 cases of soda. Each case has 24 cans. Which number sentence should be used to find how many cans of soda he bought in all?

Ⓕ $24 - 6 = \square$

Ⓖ $6 + 24 = \square$

Ⓗ $6 \times 24 = \square$

Ⓙ $24 \div 6 = \square$

Ⓚ NG

GO ON ⇨

Practice Test 3 (continued)

21. Tim has a job as a baby-sitter. Last week he baby-sat for 5 hours. What else do you need to know to find how much money Tim made?

Ⓐ the name of the family he worked for

Ⓑ how much he was paid per hour

Ⓒ where he baby-sat

Ⓓ how many kids he baby-sat

Ⓔ NG

22. Mrs. Jones bought these things at the store.

$24.50   **$8.00**

She gave the clerk $40.00. How much change should she get?

Ⓕ $6.50

Ⓖ $7.50

Ⓗ $16.50

Ⓙ $32.50

Ⓚ NG

23. Joey weighed 100 pounds on January 1st. He gained 6 pounds in January and 5 pounds in February. In March he lost 4 pounds. How much did Joey weigh at the end of March?

Ⓐ 101 pounds

Ⓑ 108 pounds

Ⓒ 111 pounds

Ⓓ 115 pounds

Ⓔ NG

24. A group of children went to the aquarium. There were 7 children in one van and 8 children in another van.

Tickets for the aquarium were $4.00 each.

How much did the tickets cost for all the children together?

Ⓕ $15.00

Ⓖ $19.00

Ⓗ $40.00

Ⓙ $60.00

Ⓚ NG

STOP

Student Name _____ Grade _____

Teacher Name _____ Date _____

MATHEMATICS

1 Ⓐ Ⓑ Ⓒ Ⓓ Ⓔ	11 Ⓐ Ⓑ Ⓒ Ⓓ Ⓔ	21 Ⓐ Ⓑ Ⓒ Ⓓ Ⓔ	31 Ⓐ Ⓑ Ⓒ Ⓓ Ⓔ
2 Ⓕ Ⓖ Ⓗ Ⓙ Ⓚ	12 Ⓕ Ⓖ Ⓗ Ⓙ Ⓚ	22 Ⓕ Ⓖ Ⓗ Ⓙ Ⓚ	32 Ⓕ Ⓖ Ⓗ Ⓙ Ⓚ
3 Ⓐ Ⓑ Ⓒ Ⓓ Ⓔ	13 Ⓐ Ⓑ Ⓒ Ⓓ Ⓔ	23 Ⓐ Ⓑ Ⓒ Ⓓ Ⓔ	33 Ⓐ Ⓑ Ⓒ Ⓓ Ⓔ
4 Ⓕ Ⓖ Ⓗ Ⓙ Ⓚ	14 Ⓕ Ⓖ Ⓗ Ⓙ Ⓚ	24 Ⓕ Ⓖ Ⓗ Ⓙ Ⓚ	34 Ⓕ Ⓖ Ⓗ Ⓙ Ⓚ
5 Ⓐ Ⓑ Ⓒ Ⓓ Ⓔ	15 Ⓐ Ⓑ Ⓒ Ⓓ Ⓔ	25 Ⓐ Ⓑ Ⓒ Ⓓ Ⓔ	35 Ⓐ Ⓑ Ⓒ Ⓓ Ⓔ
6 Ⓕ Ⓖ Ⓗ Ⓙ Ⓚ	16 Ⓕ Ⓖ Ⓗ Ⓙ Ⓚ	26 Ⓕ Ⓖ Ⓗ Ⓙ Ⓚ	36 Ⓕ Ⓖ Ⓗ Ⓙ Ⓚ
7 Ⓐ Ⓑ Ⓒ Ⓓ Ⓔ	17 Ⓐ Ⓑ Ⓒ Ⓓ Ⓔ	27 Ⓐ Ⓑ Ⓒ Ⓓ Ⓔ	37 Ⓐ Ⓑ Ⓒ Ⓓ Ⓔ
8 Ⓕ Ⓖ Ⓗ Ⓙ Ⓚ	18 Ⓕ Ⓖ Ⓗ Ⓙ Ⓚ	28 Ⓕ Ⓖ Ⓗ Ⓙ Ⓚ	38 Ⓕ Ⓖ Ⓗ Ⓙ Ⓚ
9 Ⓐ Ⓑ Ⓒ Ⓓ Ⓔ	19 Ⓐ Ⓑ Ⓒ Ⓓ Ⓔ	29 Ⓐ Ⓑ Ⓒ Ⓓ Ⓔ	39 Ⓐ Ⓑ Ⓒ Ⓓ Ⓔ
10 Ⓕ Ⓖ Ⓗ Ⓙ Ⓚ	20 Ⓕ Ⓖ Ⓗ Ⓙ Ⓚ	30 Ⓕ Ⓖ Ⓗ Ⓙ Ⓚ	40 Ⓕ Ⓖ Ⓗ Ⓙ Ⓚ

Practice
Test 4

Computation

Practice Test 4

Directions. Choose the best answer to each question. Mark your answer. If the correct answer is *not given,* choose "NG."

1.
$$58 + 43$$

- (A) 91
- (B) 92
- (C) 95
- (D) 101
- (E) NG

2.
$$215 + 67$$

- (F) 292
- (G) 282
- (H) 281
- (J) 272
- (K) NG

3.
$$83 - 19$$

- (A) 63
- (B) 64
- (C) 74
- (D) 76
- (E) NG

4. This chart shows the number of shirts sold at a clothing store in one day.

Shirts Sold	
T-shirts	12
Boys' Shirts	20
Sweatshirts	8
Girls' Shirts	14

How many shirts were sold in all that day?

- (F) 32
- (G) 40
- (H) 42
- (J) 54
- (K) NG

5. Jesse raked leaves for three of her neighbors. This list shows how much they paid her.

Mrs. Jones	$15
Mr. Peters	$34
Ms. Kline	$28

How much did Jesse make all together?

- (A) $67
- (B) $76
- (C) $78
- (D) $87
- (E) NG

GO ON

Practice Test 4 (continued)

6.
$$248 \\ -\,95$$

   Ⓕ 343
   Ⓖ 163
   Ⓗ 153
   Ⓙ 152
   Ⓚ NG

7. $6 \times 5 = \Box$

   Ⓐ 24
   Ⓑ 28
   Ⓒ 30
   Ⓓ 35
   Ⓔ NG

8.
$$42 \\ \times\,3$$

   Ⓕ 18
   Ⓖ 26
   Ⓗ 45
   Ⓙ 125
   Ⓚ NG

9. $28 \times 10 = \Box$

   Ⓐ 280
   Ⓑ 281
   Ⓒ 290
   Ⓓ 2810
   Ⓔ NG

10. The chart shows the number of boys who went to swim lessons each day.

Boys at Swim Lessons	
Monday	6
Wednesday	9
Friday	15

What was the average number of boys at swim lessons each day?

   Ⓕ 30
   Ⓖ 10
   Ⓗ 7
   Ⓙ 6
   Ⓚ NG

11. This chart shows how many kids in a third-grade class have birthdays in each season.

Season	Number of Birthdays
Winter	4
Spring	9
Summer	8
Fall	15

If you choose only one of these kids, his or her birthday is most likely to be in the —

   Ⓐ winter   Ⓒ summer
   Ⓑ spring   Ⓓ fall

Practice Test 4 *(continued)*

12. 6)‾42‾

 (F) 4
 (G) 5
 (H) 6
 (J) 7
 (K) NG

13. $18 \div 3 = \square$

 (A) 3
 (B) 4
 (C) 5
 (D) 8
 (E) NG

14. $\dfrac{1}{4}$
 $+\ \dfrac{1}{4}$

 (F) $\dfrac{2}{8}$
 (G) $\dfrac{1}{8}$
 (H) $\dfrac{1}{2}$
 (J) $\dfrac{1}{3}$
 (K) NG

15. Hank has 3 pairs of socks and 4 pairs of sneakers.

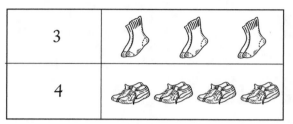

How many different combinations of 1 pair of socks and 1 pair of sneakers can he make?

 (A) 15
 (B) 12
 (C) 7
 (D) 3
 (E) NG

16. Jenna has these candies in a bag.

If she takes one candy without looking, what kind is it most likely to be?

 (F)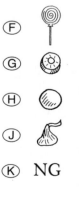

 (G)

 (H)

 (J)

 (K) NG

GO ON ⇨

Practice Test 4 *(continued)*

17. $\frac{2}{3} - \frac{1}{3} = \square$

    Ⓐ $\frac{1}{3}$

    Ⓑ $\frac{3}{6}$

    Ⓒ $\frac{1}{6}$

    Ⓓ $\frac{2}{9}$

    Ⓔ NG

18. $\begin{array}{r} \$6.50 \\ + \ 3.75 \\ \hline \end{array}$

    Ⓕ $10.75

    Ⓖ $10.25

    Ⓗ $9.25

    Ⓙ $3.25

    Ⓚ NG

19. $1.2 + 3.4 = \square$

    Ⓐ 2.2

    Ⓑ 3.6

    Ⓒ 4.6

    Ⓓ 4.8

    Ⓔ NG

20. Ms. Goble had $50.00. She spent $23.00. How much money did she have left?

    Ⓕ $16.50

    Ⓖ $20.25

    Ⓗ $25.50

    Ⓙ $27.00

    Ⓚ NG

21. Mickey rode 8.4 miles on his bike in the morning. Then he rode 5.5 miles in the afternoon.

| 8.4 miles | Morning |

| 5.5 miles | Afternoon |

How far did Mickey ride in all?

    Ⓐ 3.9 miles

    Ⓑ 4.9 miles

    Ⓒ 13.1 miles

    Ⓓ 13.9 miles

    Ⓔ NG

Scholastic Inc.

Practice Test 4 *(continued)*

22. $6 + \square = 15$

What number goes in the box to make the sentence true?

- Ⓕ 7
- Ⓖ 8
- Ⓗ 9
- Ⓙ 10
- Ⓚ NG

23. $12 - n = 10$

What is the value of *n?*

- Ⓐ 2
- Ⓑ 3
- Ⓒ 4
- Ⓓ 5
- Ⓔ NG

24. $7 \times \square = 21$

What number goes in the box?

- Ⓕ 2
- Ⓖ 3
- Ⓗ 4
- Ⓙ 6
- Ⓚ NG

Use the grid below to answer questions 25 and 26.

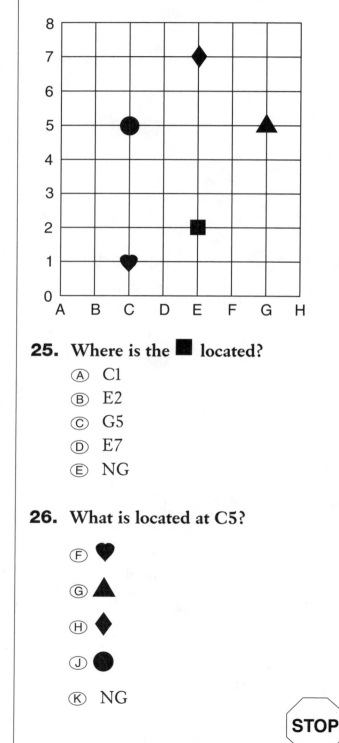

25. Where is the ■ located?

- Ⓐ C1
- Ⓑ E2
- Ⓒ G5
- Ⓓ E7
- Ⓔ NG

26. What is located at C5?

- Ⓕ ♥
- Ⓖ ▲
- Ⓗ ◆
- Ⓙ ●
- Ⓚ NG

STOP

Scholastic Inc.

ANSWER SHEET

Student Name _____ Grade _____

Teacher Name _____ Date _____

MATHEMATICS

1 Ⓐ Ⓑ Ⓒ Ⓓ Ⓔ	11 Ⓐ Ⓑ Ⓒ Ⓓ Ⓔ	21 Ⓐ Ⓑ Ⓒ Ⓓ Ⓔ	31 Ⓐ Ⓑ Ⓒ Ⓓ Ⓔ
2 Ⓕ Ⓖ Ⓗ Ⓙ Ⓚ	12 Ⓕ Ⓖ Ⓗ Ⓙ Ⓚ	22 Ⓕ Ⓖ Ⓗ Ⓙ Ⓚ	32 Ⓕ Ⓖ Ⓗ Ⓙ Ⓚ
3 Ⓐ Ⓑ Ⓒ Ⓓ Ⓔ	13 Ⓐ Ⓑ Ⓒ Ⓓ Ⓔ	23 Ⓐ Ⓑ Ⓒ Ⓓ Ⓔ	33 Ⓐ Ⓑ Ⓒ Ⓓ Ⓔ
4 Ⓕ Ⓖ Ⓗ Ⓙ Ⓚ	14 Ⓕ Ⓖ Ⓗ Ⓙ Ⓚ	24 Ⓕ Ⓖ Ⓗ Ⓙ Ⓚ	34 Ⓕ Ⓖ Ⓗ Ⓙ Ⓚ
5 Ⓐ Ⓑ Ⓒ Ⓓ Ⓔ	15 Ⓐ Ⓑ Ⓒ Ⓓ Ⓔ	25 Ⓐ Ⓑ Ⓒ Ⓓ Ⓔ	35 Ⓐ Ⓑ Ⓒ Ⓓ Ⓔ
6 Ⓕ Ⓖ Ⓗ Ⓙ Ⓚ	16 Ⓕ Ⓖ Ⓗ Ⓙ Ⓚ	26 Ⓕ Ⓖ Ⓗ Ⓙ Ⓚ	36 Ⓕ Ⓖ Ⓗ Ⓙ Ⓚ
7 Ⓐ Ⓑ Ⓒ Ⓓ Ⓔ	17 Ⓐ Ⓑ Ⓒ Ⓓ Ⓔ	27 Ⓐ Ⓑ Ⓒ Ⓓ Ⓔ	37 Ⓐ Ⓑ Ⓒ Ⓓ Ⓔ
8 Ⓕ Ⓖ Ⓗ Ⓙ Ⓚ	18 Ⓕ Ⓖ Ⓗ Ⓙ Ⓚ	28 Ⓕ Ⓖ Ⓗ Ⓙ Ⓚ	38 Ⓕ Ⓖ Ⓗ Ⓙ Ⓚ
9 Ⓐ Ⓑ Ⓒ Ⓓ Ⓔ	19 Ⓐ Ⓑ Ⓒ Ⓓ Ⓔ	29 Ⓐ Ⓑ Ⓒ Ⓓ Ⓔ	39 Ⓐ Ⓑ Ⓒ Ⓓ Ⓔ
10 Ⓕ Ⓖ Ⓗ Ⓙ Ⓚ	20 Ⓕ Ⓖ Ⓗ Ⓙ Ⓚ	30 Ⓕ Ⓖ Ⓗ Ⓙ Ⓚ	40 Ⓕ Ⓖ Ⓗ Ⓙ Ⓚ

Practice
Test 5

Numeration and
Number Concepts

Practice Test 5

Directions. Choose the best answer to each question. Mark your answer.

1. Mr. Crowley was counting pairs of children on a school bus.

   . . . 6, 8, 10, 12, _____

   Which number should come next?
   Ⓐ 13
   Ⓑ 14
   Ⓒ 15
   Ⓓ 16

2. There are 10 flowers in each bunch.

   How many flowers are there in all?
   Ⓕ 8
   Ⓖ 50
   Ⓗ 53
   Ⓙ 54

3. Ms. Grimes wrote a check for three thousand nine hundred ten dollars. Which number means three thousand nine hundred ten?
   Ⓐ 3091
   Ⓑ 3901
   Ⓒ 3910
   Ⓓ 30,910

4. Cheaha Mountain in Alabama is 2405 feet high. What is that number in words?
   Ⓕ two thousand four hundred five
   Ⓖ two thousand forty-five
   Ⓗ two thousand four hundred fifty
   Ⓙ two hundred forty-five

5. Which address is an even number?

   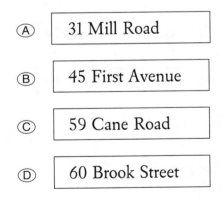

   Ⓐ 31 Mill Road
   Ⓑ 45 First Avenue
   Ⓒ 59 Cane Road
   Ⓓ 60 Brook Street

   GO ON

Practice Test 5 *(continued)*

6. The chart shows the length of four bridges in Texas.

Bridge	Length (feet)
Neches River	640
Trinity River	480
Ship Channel	630
Gulfgate	664

Which bridge is longest?

ⓕ Neches River

ⓖ Trinity River

ⓗ Ship Channel

ⓙ Gulfgate

7. The chart shows the height of four dams in the United States.

Dam	Height (feet)
Dworshak	718
Glen Canyon	708
Hoover	725
Oroville	754

Which dam is highest?

Ⓐ Dworshak

Ⓑ Glen Canyon

Ⓒ Hoover

Ⓓ Oroville

8. Which number means 2000 + 70 + 3?

ⓕ 273

ⓖ 2073

ⓗ 2703

ⓙ 20,703

9. A total of 2945 people went to a hockey game. What does the **4** stand for in **2945**?

Ⓐ 4 thousands

Ⓑ 4 hundreds

Ⓒ 4 tens

Ⓓ 4 ones

10. There are 3722 people living in the town of Wingate. What is that number rounded to the nearest hundred?

ⓕ 3000

ⓖ 3700

ⓗ 3800

ⓙ 4000

Scholastic Inc.

Practice Test 5 *(continued)*

11. Mrs. Welles is making a quilt with this pattern.

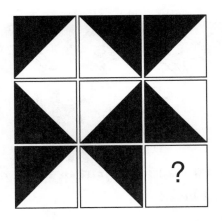

What goes in the blank square to complete the pattern?

Ⓐ 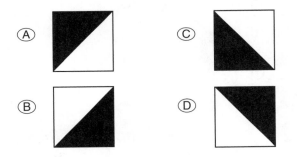 Ⓒ

Ⓑ Ⓓ

12. Doreen made this number pattern.

2, 7, 12, 17, _____

If the same pattern continues, what number should come next?

Ⓕ 18
Ⓖ 20
Ⓗ 22
Ⓙ 24

13. Which sign has an odd number?

Ⓐ SPEED LIMIT **60** Ⓒ BOSTON 31 MILES

Ⓑ PAY TOLL 500 FEET Ⓓ Walton pop. 48

14. Which number is marked on the number line?

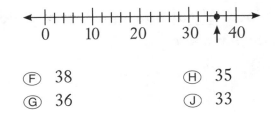

Ⓕ 38   Ⓗ 35
Ⓖ 36   Ⓙ 33

15. Dolly's Bakery sold 512 muffins on Friday and 684 muffins on Saturday. **About** how many muffins were sold in those two days?

Ⓐ 1200
Ⓑ 1400
Ⓒ 1600
Ⓓ 1800

GO ON

Scholastic Inc.

Practice Test 5 *(continued)*

16. What number is shown on the number line?

  300   400   500

- (F) 342
- (G) 402
- (H) 412
- (J) 420

17. Becca got $97.00 for her birthday. She spent $48.00 for a new baseball glove. **About** how much money did she have left?

- (A) $100
- (B) $50
- (C) $30
- (D) $10

18. Which is another way to write 8 + 8 + 8?

- (F) 3 × 8
- (G) 8 + 3
- (H) 8 × 8 × 8
- (J) 24 + 8

19. Polly got these black and white fish at the pet shop.

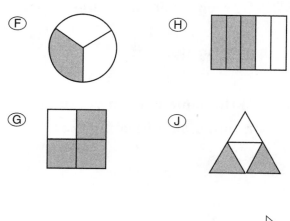

What fractional part of these fish are black?

- (A) $\frac{3}{5}$
- (B) $\frac{2}{3}$
- (C) $\frac{1}{2}$
- (D) $\frac{2}{5}$

20. Which figure shows $\frac{3}{4}$ shaded?

- (F)
- (H)
- (G)
- (J)

GO ON

Scholastic Inc.

Practice Test 5 *(continued)*

21. Which number goes in the box to make this number sentence true?

$9 \times 0 = \square$

(A) 0

(B) 1

(C) 9

(D) 90

22. Which number sentence goes with this fact?

$5 + 3 = 8$

(F) $5 - 3 = 2$

(G) $8 + 3 = 11$

(H) $8 - 8 = 0$

(J) $8 - 5 = 3$

23. Which number sentence is true?

(A) $4 \times 0 = 4$

(B) $4 \times 1 = 4$

(C) $4 - 0 = 0$

(D) $4 + 0 = 1 + 4$

24. This sign shows the lengths of four hiking trails.

Moose Trail $\frac{1}{2}$ mile

Elk Trail $\frac{2}{3}$ mile

Deer Trail $\frac{1}{8}$ mile

Bear Trail $\frac{3}{4}$ mile

Which lists the four trails in order from shortest to longest?

(F) Deer, Moose, Elk, Bear

(G) Moose, Elk, Bear, Deer

(H) Bear, Elk, Moose, Deer

(J) Deer, Elk, Bear, Moose

25. Which bag of peanuts weighs most?

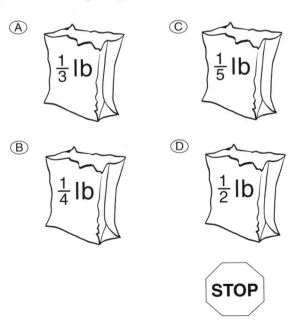

(A) $\frac{1}{3}$ lb

(C) $\frac{1}{5}$ lb

(B) $\frac{1}{4}$ lb

(D) $\frac{1}{2}$ lb

STOP

ANSWER SHEET

Practice Test # 5

Student Name _____ Grade _____

Teacher Name _____ Date _____

MATHEMATICS

1 Ⓐ Ⓑ Ⓒ Ⓓ Ⓔ	11 Ⓐ Ⓑ Ⓒ Ⓓ Ⓔ	21 Ⓐ Ⓑ Ⓒ Ⓓ Ⓔ	31 Ⓐ Ⓑ Ⓒ Ⓓ Ⓔ
2 Ⓕ Ⓖ Ⓗ Ⓙ Ⓚ	12 Ⓕ Ⓖ Ⓗ Ⓙ Ⓚ	22 Ⓕ Ⓖ Ⓗ Ⓙ Ⓚ	32 Ⓕ Ⓖ Ⓗ Ⓙ Ⓚ
3 Ⓐ Ⓑ Ⓒ Ⓓ Ⓔ	13 Ⓐ Ⓑ Ⓒ Ⓓ Ⓔ	23 Ⓐ Ⓑ Ⓒ Ⓓ Ⓔ	33 Ⓐ Ⓑ Ⓒ Ⓓ Ⓔ
4 Ⓕ Ⓖ Ⓗ Ⓙ Ⓚ	14 Ⓕ Ⓖ Ⓗ Ⓙ Ⓚ	24 Ⓕ Ⓖ Ⓗ Ⓙ Ⓚ	34 Ⓕ Ⓖ Ⓗ Ⓙ Ⓚ
5 Ⓐ Ⓑ Ⓒ Ⓓ Ⓔ	15 Ⓐ Ⓑ Ⓒ Ⓓ Ⓔ	25 Ⓐ Ⓑ Ⓒ Ⓓ Ⓔ	35 Ⓐ Ⓑ Ⓒ Ⓓ Ⓔ
6 Ⓕ Ⓖ Ⓗ Ⓙ Ⓚ	16 Ⓕ Ⓖ Ⓗ Ⓙ Ⓚ	26 Ⓕ Ⓖ Ⓗ Ⓙ Ⓚ	36 Ⓕ Ⓖ Ⓗ Ⓙ Ⓚ
7 Ⓐ Ⓑ Ⓒ Ⓓ Ⓔ	17 Ⓐ Ⓑ Ⓒ Ⓓ Ⓔ	27 Ⓐ Ⓑ Ⓒ Ⓓ Ⓔ	37 Ⓐ Ⓑ Ⓒ Ⓓ Ⓔ
8 Ⓕ Ⓖ Ⓗ Ⓙ Ⓚ	18 Ⓕ Ⓖ Ⓗ Ⓙ Ⓚ	28 Ⓕ Ⓖ Ⓗ Ⓙ Ⓚ	38 Ⓕ Ⓖ Ⓗ Ⓙ Ⓚ
9 Ⓐ Ⓑ Ⓒ Ⓓ Ⓔ	19 Ⓐ Ⓑ Ⓒ Ⓓ Ⓔ	29 Ⓐ Ⓑ Ⓒ Ⓓ Ⓔ	39 Ⓐ Ⓑ Ⓒ Ⓓ Ⓔ
10 Ⓕ Ⓖ Ⓗ Ⓙ Ⓚ	20 Ⓕ Ⓖ Ⓗ Ⓙ Ⓚ	30 Ⓕ Ⓖ Ⓗ Ⓙ Ⓚ	40 Ⓕ Ⓖ Ⓗ Ⓙ Ⓚ

Practice Test 6

Geometry and Measurement

Practice Test 6

Directions. Choose the best answer to each question. Mark your answer.

1. Which figure is a rectangle?

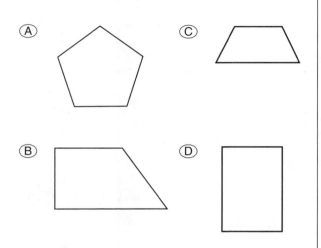

Ⓐ   Ⓒ

Ⓑ   Ⓓ

2. Which two figures are the same size and shape?

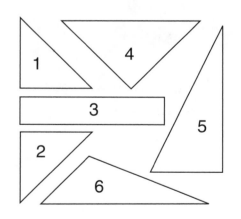

Ⓕ 1 and 2
Ⓖ 3 and 6
Ⓗ 5 and 6
Ⓙ 4 and 5

3. Which is shaped like a cone?

Ⓐ   Ⓒ

Ⓑ   Ⓓ

4. If you fold each figure on the dotted line, in which figure will the two halves match exactly?

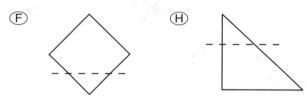

Ⓕ   Ⓗ

Ⓖ   Ⓙ

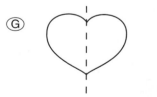
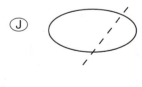

 GO ON

Practice Test 6 *(continued)*

5. Fran made this square.

How many of these squares will fit into this figure?

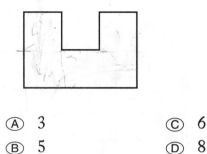

Ⓐ 3　　Ⓒ 6

Ⓑ 5　　Ⓓ 8

6. Jared has these coins in his pocket.

How much money does Jared have in his pocket?

Ⓕ 28¢

Ⓖ 37¢

Ⓗ 42¢

Ⓙ 46¢

7. May Li got this much change back at the store.

How much change did she get?

Ⓐ $1.30

Ⓑ $2.06

Ⓒ $2.30

Ⓓ $2.35

8. What is the area of this figure (in square units)?

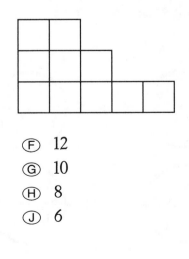

Ⓕ 12

Ⓖ 10

Ⓗ 8

Ⓙ 6

GO ON

Scholastic Inc.

Practice Test 6 *(continued)*

9. Glen woke up at the time shown on the clock.

What time did Glen wake up?

Ⓐ 6:45

Ⓑ 7:00

Ⓒ 7:15

Ⓓ 7:45

10. Debbie's swim lessons started at the time shown on the clock.

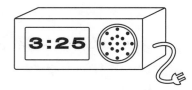

Which clock face shows the same time?

11. Which unit should be used to measure the length of a classroom?

Ⓐ miles

Ⓑ pounds

Ⓒ feet

Ⓓ gallons

12. Danny put some milk in a bowl for his cat. If he measured the amount of milk in the bowl, it would be about —

Ⓕ 5 ounces

Ⓖ 5 cups

Ⓗ 5 yards

Ⓙ 5 quarts

13. How long is the pencil? (Use your inch ruler.)

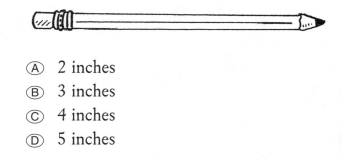

Ⓐ 2 inches

Ⓑ 3 inches

Ⓒ 4 inches

Ⓓ 5 inches

Scholastic Inc.

Practice Test 6 (continued)

14. How long is the stick of gum?
(Use your centimeter ruler.)

    Ⓕ 5 centimeters

    Ⓖ 6 centimeters

    Ⓗ 7 centimeters

    Ⓙ 8 centimeters

15. On the first day of winter, Norman looked at a thermometer. The thermometer looked like the one shown below.

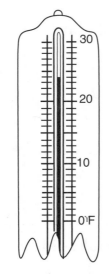

What was the temperature?

    Ⓐ 36°F

    Ⓑ 34°F

    Ⓒ 28°F

    Ⓓ 24°F

16. Hannah went swimming in the lake on a summer day. What was most likely the temperature that day?

    Ⓕ 32°F   Ⓗ 60°F

    Ⓖ 40°F   Ⓙ 85°F

17. Where is the ◆ located on the grid?

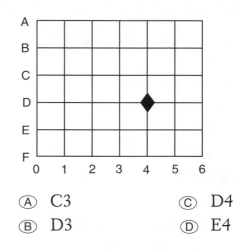

    Ⓐ C3   Ⓒ D4

    Ⓑ D3   Ⓓ E4

18. This tile was turned on its side in the direction of the arrow.

Which picture shows the tile after it was turned?

    Ⓕ    Ⓗ

    Ⓖ   Ⓙ

Practice Test 6 *(continued)*

19. Look at the calendar.

June						
Sun	Mon	Tue	Wed	Thu	Fri	Sat
					1	2
3	4	5	6	7	8	9
10	11	12	13	14	15	16
17	18	19	20	21	22	23
24	25	26	27	28	29	30

What day of the week is June 20?

Ⓐ Monday

Ⓑ Tuesday

Ⓒ Wednesday

Ⓓ Saturday

20. Jerry made this tally chart to keep track of the fish he caught in one month.

Kind of Fish	Number of Fish
Sunfish	⊦⊦⊦⊦ ⊦⊦⊦⊦ I
Perch	⊦⊦⊦⊦ ⊦⊦⊦⊦ ⊦⊦⊦⊦ I
Trout	⊦⊦⊦⊦ II
Bass	⊦⊦⊦⊦ IIII

How many perch did he catch?

Ⓕ 16

Ⓖ 11

Ⓗ 9

Ⓙ 7

Adele made a graph to show how many books she read each week. Use the graph to answer questions 21 and 22.

Books Read

21. In which week did Adele read the most books?

Ⓐ Week 2

Ⓑ Week 3

Ⓒ Week 4

Ⓓ Week 5

22. How many books did she read in Week 2?

Ⓕ 5

Ⓖ 4

Ⓗ 3

Ⓙ 2

STOP

Scholastic Inc.

ANSWER SHEET

Practice Test # 6

Student Name _____ Grade _____

Teacher Name _____ Date _____

MATHEMATICS

1 Ⓐ Ⓑ Ⓒ Ⓓ Ⓔ	11 Ⓐ Ⓑ Ⓒ Ⓓ Ⓔ	21 Ⓐ Ⓑ Ⓒ Ⓓ Ⓔ	31 Ⓐ Ⓑ Ⓒ Ⓓ Ⓔ
2 Ⓕ Ⓖ Ⓗ Ⓙ Ⓚ	12 Ⓕ Ⓖ Ⓗ Ⓙ Ⓚ	22 Ⓕ Ⓖ Ⓗ Ⓙ Ⓚ	32 Ⓕ Ⓖ Ⓗ Ⓙ Ⓚ
3 Ⓐ Ⓑ Ⓒ Ⓓ Ⓔ	13 Ⓐ Ⓑ Ⓒ Ⓓ Ⓔ	23 Ⓐ Ⓑ Ⓒ Ⓓ Ⓔ	33 Ⓐ Ⓑ Ⓒ Ⓓ Ⓔ
4 Ⓕ Ⓖ Ⓗ Ⓙ Ⓚ	14 Ⓕ Ⓖ Ⓗ Ⓙ Ⓚ	24 Ⓕ Ⓖ Ⓗ Ⓙ Ⓚ	34 Ⓕ Ⓖ Ⓗ Ⓙ Ⓚ
5 Ⓐ Ⓑ Ⓒ Ⓓ Ⓔ	15 Ⓐ Ⓑ Ⓒ Ⓓ Ⓔ	25 Ⓐ Ⓑ Ⓒ Ⓓ Ⓔ	35 Ⓐ Ⓑ Ⓒ Ⓓ Ⓔ
6 Ⓕ Ⓖ Ⓗ Ⓙ Ⓚ	16 Ⓕ Ⓖ Ⓗ Ⓙ Ⓚ	26 Ⓕ Ⓖ Ⓗ Ⓙ Ⓚ	36 Ⓕ Ⓖ Ⓗ Ⓙ Ⓚ
7 Ⓐ Ⓑ Ⓒ Ⓓ Ⓔ	17 Ⓐ Ⓑ Ⓒ Ⓓ Ⓔ	27 Ⓐ Ⓑ Ⓒ Ⓓ Ⓔ	37 Ⓐ Ⓑ Ⓒ Ⓓ Ⓔ
8 Ⓕ Ⓖ Ⓗ Ⓙ Ⓚ	18 Ⓕ Ⓖ Ⓗ Ⓙ Ⓚ	28 Ⓕ Ⓖ Ⓗ Ⓙ Ⓚ	38 Ⓕ Ⓖ Ⓗ Ⓙ Ⓚ
9 Ⓐ Ⓑ Ⓒ Ⓓ Ⓔ	19 Ⓐ Ⓑ Ⓒ Ⓓ Ⓔ	29 Ⓐ Ⓑ Ⓒ Ⓓ Ⓔ	39 Ⓐ Ⓑ Ⓒ Ⓓ Ⓔ
10 Ⓕ Ⓖ Ⓗ Ⓙ Ⓚ	20 Ⓕ Ⓖ Ⓗ Ⓙ Ⓚ	30 Ⓕ Ⓖ Ⓗ Ⓙ Ⓚ	40 Ⓕ Ⓖ Ⓗ Ⓙ Ⓚ

Practice
Test 7

Problem Solving

Practice Test 7

Directions. Choose the best answer to each question. Mark your answer. If the correct answer is *not given,* choose "NG."

1. At a pet show, there were 119 dogs and 85 cats.

119   85

How many animals in all were at the pet show?

Ⓐ 214

Ⓑ 204

Ⓒ 198

Ⓓ 194

Ⓔ NG

2. On Tuesday, a restaurant served 64 customers at breakfast and 78 customers at lunch. How many customers were served all together on Tuesday?

Ⓕ 132

Ⓖ 134

Ⓗ 142

Ⓙ 148

Ⓚ NG

3. Mike has these videos at home.

Cartoons	15
Movies	8
Sports	11

How many videos does he have in all?

Ⓐ 19

Ⓑ 23

Ⓒ 26

Ⓓ 35

Ⓔ NG

4. A line of 430 people wanted to buy tickets for a dance show. Only 385 people got tickets. How many people did <u>not</u> get tickets?

Ⓕ 35

Ⓖ 45

Ⓗ 55

Ⓙ 815

Ⓚ NG

5. Carol is reading a book that is 360 pages long. She has read 219 pages so far. How many pages does she have left to read?

Ⓐ 579

Ⓑ 159

Ⓒ 141

Ⓓ 131

Ⓔ NG

GO ON ⟩

Practice Test 7 *(continued)*

6. Glenn exercises for 25 minutes each day for 5 days each week. How much time does he spend exercising each week?

Ⓕ 30 minutes

Ⓖ 105 minutes

Ⓗ 120 minutes

Ⓙ 125 minutes

Ⓚ NG

7. A school has 6 vans, and 7 students can ride in each van. How many students in all can ride in the vans?

Ⓐ 48

Ⓑ 42

Ⓒ 35

Ⓓ 13

Ⓔ NG

8. Mr. Matthews has 28 chairs. He wants to put all the chairs in 4 rows with an equal number of chairs in each row. How many chairs will be in each row?

Ⓕ 5

Ⓖ 6

Ⓗ 8

Ⓙ 9

Ⓚ NG

9. Kiki bought lunch for $8.57. She paid for it with a $10-dollar bill. How much change should she get?

Ⓐ $1.48

Ⓑ $1.46

Ⓒ $1.38

Ⓓ $0.48

Ⓔ NG

10. Kent bought a roll of film for $6.25. The tax was $0.38.

$6.25

Tax $0.38

What was the total cost for the roll of film?

Ⓕ $5.87

Ⓖ $6.53

Ⓗ $6.63

Ⓙ $6.73

Ⓚ NG

Practice Test 7 (continued)

11. Mr. Bunker fell asleep at the time shown.

He woke up 1 hour 30 minutes later. What time did he wake up?

Ⓐ 4:45

Ⓑ 5:15

Ⓒ 5:30

Ⓓ 5:45

Ⓔ NG

12. Mrs. Coombs is watching a TV show that lasts 60 minutes. She has been watching for 48 minutes. How much longer will the show last?

Ⓕ 10 minutes

Ⓖ 14 minutes

Ⓗ 22 minutes

Ⓙ 24 minutes

Ⓚ NG

13. Micah bought these things at the hardware store.

$6.09 $9.85 $3.94

<u>About</u> how much did he spend in all?

Ⓐ $10

Ⓑ $15

Ⓒ $20

Ⓓ $30

14. Lonnie bought 4 packs of playing cards. Each pack has 52 cards. <u>About</u> how many cards did he buy in all?

Ⓕ 50   Ⓗ 150

Ⓖ 100   Ⓙ 200

15. Mrs. Lopez is making 205 cupcakes for a bake sale. She has made 68 cupcakes so far. <u>About</u> how many more cupcakes does she have to make?

Ⓐ 170   Ⓒ 90

Ⓑ 130   Ⓓ 70

GO ON

Practice Test 7 *(continued)*

16. Look at the spinner.

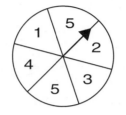

If you spin the spinner once, what number will it most likely land on?

Ⓕ 5

Ⓖ 4

Ⓗ 3

Ⓙ 2

Ⓚ NG

17. Pete has these toy ducks in a pool.

Color	Number of Ducks
Yellow	15
White	8
Black	7
Red	6
Blue	10

If Pete takes one duck out of the pool without looking, he is most likely to get which color?

Ⓐ yellow

Ⓑ white

Ⓒ black

Ⓓ blue

Ⓔ NG

18. Manny is 48 inches tall. He is 3 inches taller than Kim. Ashley is 3 inches shorter than Kim. How tall is Ashley?

Ⓕ 46 inches

Ⓖ 45 inches

Ⓗ 42 inches

Ⓙ 39 inches

Ⓚ NG

19. Tara cut 47 red roses. She sold 28 of them. Which number sentence should be used to find how many roses she had left?

Ⓐ $47 + 28 = \square$

Ⓑ $28 - 47 = \square$

Ⓒ $47 \times 28 = \square$

Ⓓ $47 \div 28 = \square$

Ⓔ NG

20. Josh bought 5 boxes of golf balls. Each box had 12 balls. Which number sentence should be used to find how many golf balls he bought in all?

Ⓕ $12 + 5 = \square$

Ⓖ $5 \times 12 = \square$

Ⓗ $12 - 5 = \square$

Ⓙ $5 + 12 = \square$

Ⓚ NG

GO ON

Practice Test 7 *(continued)*

21. Karen has a job as a dishwasher in a restaurant. Last week she made a total of $228.00. What else do you need to know to find how much Karen makes per hour?

ⓐ the name of the restaurant

ⓑ what days she works

ⓒ when she started her job

ⓓ how many hours she worked

ⓔ NG

22. Mr. Ames bought these things at the store.

$25.00 $8.50

He gave the clerk $50.00. How much change should he get?

ⓕ $16.50

ⓖ $17.50

ⓗ $25.00

ⓙ $33.50

ⓚ NG

23. Pam had 120 stamps in her stamp collection. She bought 12 new stamps on Thursday and 20 new stamps on Saturday. Then she sold 8 of her stamps. How many stamps did she have left in her collection?

ⓐ 132

ⓑ 140

ⓒ 144

ⓓ 152

ⓔ NG

24. A family of 2 adults and 3 children went to the movies. Tickets for adults were $7.00 each. Tickets for children were $4.00 each.

2   Adult $7.00

3   Child $4.00

How much did the family pay in all for their tickets?

ⓕ $12.00

ⓖ $14.00

ⓗ $26.00

ⓙ $28.00

ⓚ NG

STOP

ANSWER SHEET

Student Name _____ Grade _____

Teacher Name _____ Date _____

MATHEMATICS

1 Ⓐ Ⓑ Ⓒ Ⓓ Ⓔ	11 Ⓐ Ⓑ Ⓒ Ⓓ Ⓔ	21 Ⓐ Ⓑ Ⓒ Ⓓ Ⓔ	31 Ⓐ Ⓑ Ⓒ Ⓓ Ⓔ
2 Ⓕ Ⓖ Ⓗ Ⓙ Ⓚ	12 Ⓕ Ⓖ Ⓗ Ⓙ Ⓚ	22 Ⓕ Ⓖ Ⓗ Ⓙ Ⓚ	32 Ⓕ Ⓖ Ⓗ Ⓙ Ⓚ
3 Ⓐ Ⓑ Ⓒ Ⓓ Ⓔ	13 Ⓐ Ⓑ Ⓒ Ⓓ Ⓔ	23 Ⓐ Ⓑ Ⓒ Ⓓ Ⓔ	33 Ⓐ Ⓑ Ⓒ Ⓓ Ⓔ
4 Ⓕ Ⓖ Ⓗ Ⓙ Ⓚ	14 Ⓕ Ⓖ Ⓗ Ⓙ Ⓚ	24 Ⓕ Ⓖ Ⓗ Ⓙ Ⓚ	34 Ⓕ Ⓖ Ⓗ Ⓙ Ⓚ
5 Ⓐ Ⓑ Ⓒ Ⓓ Ⓔ	15 Ⓐ Ⓑ Ⓒ Ⓓ Ⓔ	25 Ⓐ Ⓑ Ⓒ Ⓓ Ⓔ	35 Ⓐ Ⓑ Ⓒ Ⓓ Ⓔ
6 Ⓕ Ⓖ Ⓗ Ⓙ Ⓚ	16 Ⓕ Ⓖ Ⓗ Ⓙ Ⓚ	26 Ⓕ Ⓖ Ⓗ Ⓙ Ⓚ	36 Ⓕ Ⓖ Ⓗ Ⓙ Ⓚ
7 Ⓐ Ⓑ Ⓒ Ⓓ Ⓔ	17 Ⓐ Ⓑ Ⓒ Ⓓ Ⓔ	27 Ⓐ Ⓑ Ⓒ Ⓓ Ⓔ	37 Ⓐ Ⓑ Ⓒ Ⓓ Ⓔ
8 Ⓕ Ⓖ Ⓗ Ⓙ Ⓚ	18 Ⓕ Ⓖ Ⓗ Ⓙ Ⓚ	28 Ⓕ Ⓖ Ⓗ Ⓙ Ⓚ	38 Ⓕ Ⓖ Ⓗ Ⓙ Ⓚ
9 Ⓐ Ⓑ Ⓒ Ⓓ Ⓔ	19 Ⓐ Ⓑ Ⓒ Ⓓ Ⓔ	29 Ⓐ Ⓑ Ⓒ Ⓓ Ⓔ	39 Ⓐ Ⓑ Ⓒ Ⓓ Ⓔ
10 Ⓕ Ⓖ Ⓗ Ⓙ Ⓚ	20 Ⓕ Ⓖ Ⓗ Ⓙ Ⓚ	30 Ⓕ Ⓖ Ⓗ Ⓙ Ⓚ	40 Ⓕ Ⓖ Ⓗ Ⓙ Ⓚ

Scholastic Inc.

Practice Test 8

Computation

Practice Test 8

Directions. Choose the best answer to each question. Mark your answer. If the correct answer is *not given,* choose "NG."

1.
$$\begin{array}{r} 56 \\ + 37 \end{array}$$

- Ⓐ 81
- Ⓑ 83
- Ⓒ 93
- Ⓓ 103
- Ⓔ NG

2.
$$\begin{array}{r} 405 \\ + 98 \end{array}$$

- Ⓕ 493
- Ⓖ 501
- Ⓗ 502
- Ⓙ 513
- Ⓚ NG

3.
$$\begin{array}{r} 62 \\ - 17 \end{array}$$

- Ⓐ 44
- Ⓑ 45
- Ⓒ 55
- Ⓓ 79
- Ⓔ NG

4. This chart shows the number of vegetables picked in one day.

Vegetables Picked	
Carrots	25
Broccoli	14
Cucumbers	16
Squash	8

How many vegetables were picked in all that day?

- Ⓕ 39
- Ⓖ 53
- Ⓗ 55
- Ⓙ 63
- Ⓚ NG

5. Chuck mowed lawns for three days. This list shows what he earned.

Monday	$24
Tuesday	$28
Wednesday	$13

How much did Chuck earn all together?

- Ⓐ $62
- Ⓑ $65
- Ⓒ $76
- Ⓓ $85
- Ⓔ NG

GO ON ➡

Practice Test 8 (continued)

6.   329
       − 57

- Ⓕ 386
- Ⓖ 276
- Ⓗ 272
- Ⓙ 172
- Ⓚ NG

7.   8 × 5 = ☐

- Ⓐ 30
- Ⓑ 32
- Ⓒ 35
- Ⓓ 40
- Ⓔ NG

8.   31
       × 6

- Ⓕ 186
- Ⓖ 156
- Ⓗ 96
- Ⓙ 37
- Ⓚ NG

9.   15 × 10 = ☐

- Ⓐ 150
- Ⓑ 151
- Ⓒ 160
- Ⓓ 1510
- Ⓔ NG

10. The chart shows the number of points scored in three basketball games.

Points Scored	
Game 1	12
Game 2	8
Game 3	10

What was the average number of points scored per game?

- Ⓕ 8
- Ⓖ 10
- Ⓗ 20
- Ⓙ 30
- Ⓚ NG

11. This chart shows the number of students in a third-grade class with each color of hair.

Color	Number of Students
Black	14
Brown	8
Blond	6
Red	1

If you choose one of these students without looking, the student's hair is most likely to be —

- Ⓐ black
- Ⓒ blond
- Ⓑ brown
- Ⓓ red

Practice Test 8 (continued)

12. $7\overline{)35}$

    Ⓕ 4
    Ⓖ 5
    Ⓗ 6
    Ⓙ 7
    Ⓚ NG

13. $24 \div 4 = \square$

    Ⓐ 3
    Ⓑ 4
    Ⓒ 5
    Ⓓ 6
    Ⓔ NG

14. $\begin{array}{r} \frac{1}{2} \\ + \frac{1}{2} \\ \hline \end{array}$

    Ⓕ $\frac{1}{4}$
    Ⓖ $\frac{2}{3}$
    Ⓗ $\frac{2}{4}$
    Ⓙ $\frac{3}{4}$
    Ⓚ NG

15. Mel has 2 pairs of shorts and 5 T-shirts.

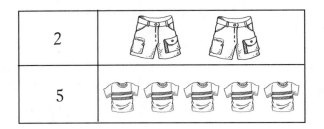

| 2 | |
| 5 | |

How many different combinations of 1 pair of shorts and 1 T-shirt can she make?

    Ⓐ 12
    Ⓑ 10
    Ⓒ 7
    Ⓓ 2
    Ⓔ NG

16. Matt has these toy rings in a bag.

Gold	6
Silver	4
Red	2
Blue	3
Green	1

If he takes one ring from the bag without looking, what color is it most likely to be?

    Ⓕ gold
    Ⓖ silver
    Ⓗ red
    Ⓙ blue
    Ⓚ NG

GO ON ▷

Scholastic Inc.

Practice Test 8 (continued)

17.

$$\frac{1}{8}$$
$$+\frac{3}{8}$$

   Ⓐ $\frac{1}{2}$

   Ⓑ $\frac{5}{8}$

   Ⓒ $\frac{4}{16}$

   Ⓓ $\frac{3}{4}$

   Ⓔ NG

18. $1\frac{1}{2} - \frac{1}{4} = \square$

   Ⓕ $\frac{1}{4}$

   Ⓖ $\frac{3}{4}$

   Ⓗ 1

   Ⓙ $1\frac{1}{4}$

   Ⓚ NG

19. $6.3 + 1.9 = \square$

   Ⓐ 7.1

   Ⓑ 7.2

   Ⓒ 8.4

   Ⓓ 8.6

   Ⓔ NG

20. Nancy had $32.50 in her piggy bank. Then she put in $4.75 more.

$+ \$4.75$

How much money did she have in all?

   Ⓕ $36.25

   Ⓖ $36.75

   Ⓗ $37.25

   Ⓙ $37.75

   Ⓚ NG

21.

Distances	
Littleton	3.2 km
Ayer	2.5 km

How much farther is Littleton than Ayer?

   Ⓐ 0.7 km

   Ⓑ 1.7 km

   Ⓒ 5.7 km

   Ⓓ 6.0 km

   Ⓔ NG

GO ON

Practice Test 8 (continued)

22. $16 + n = 25$

What is the value of n?

- (F) 41
- (G) 12
- (H) 10
- (J) 9
- (K) NG

23. **Which number goes in the box to make the number sentence true?**

$$32 - \square = 24$$

- (A) 6
- (B) 7
- (C) 8
- (D) 9
- (E) NG

24. $5 \times n = 25$

What is the value of n?

- (F) 6
- (G) 5
- (H) 4
- (J) 3
- (K) NG

Use the grid below to answer questions 25 and 26.

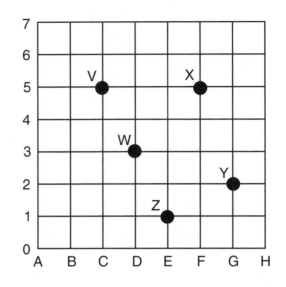

25. **What is the location of point Z?**

- (A) E1
- (B) D3
- (C) G3
- (D) C5
- (E) NG

26. **What is located at F5?**

- (F) point V
- (G) point W
- (H) point X
- (J) point Y
- (K) NG

STOP

ANSWER SHEET

Practice Test # 8

Student Name _____ Grade _____

Teacher Name _____ Date _____

MATHEMATICS

1 Ⓐ Ⓑ Ⓒ Ⓓ Ⓔ	11 Ⓐ Ⓑ Ⓒ Ⓓ Ⓔ	21 Ⓐ Ⓑ Ⓒ Ⓓ Ⓔ	31 Ⓐ Ⓑ Ⓒ Ⓓ Ⓔ
2 Ⓕ Ⓖ Ⓗ Ⓙ Ⓚ	12 Ⓕ Ⓖ Ⓗ Ⓙ Ⓚ	22 Ⓕ Ⓖ Ⓗ Ⓙ Ⓚ	32 Ⓕ Ⓖ Ⓗ Ⓙ Ⓚ
3 Ⓐ Ⓑ Ⓒ Ⓓ Ⓔ	13 Ⓐ Ⓑ Ⓒ Ⓓ Ⓔ	23 Ⓐ Ⓑ Ⓒ Ⓓ Ⓔ	33 Ⓐ Ⓑ Ⓒ Ⓓ Ⓔ
4 Ⓕ Ⓖ Ⓗ Ⓙ Ⓚ	14 Ⓕ Ⓖ Ⓗ Ⓙ Ⓚ	24 Ⓕ Ⓖ Ⓗ Ⓙ Ⓚ	34 Ⓕ Ⓖ Ⓗ Ⓙ Ⓚ
5 Ⓐ Ⓑ Ⓒ Ⓓ Ⓔ	15 Ⓐ Ⓑ Ⓒ Ⓓ Ⓔ	25 Ⓐ Ⓑ Ⓒ Ⓓ Ⓔ	35 Ⓐ Ⓑ Ⓒ Ⓓ Ⓔ
6 Ⓕ Ⓖ Ⓗ Ⓙ Ⓚ	16 Ⓕ Ⓖ Ⓗ Ⓙ Ⓚ	26 Ⓕ Ⓖ Ⓗ Ⓙ Ⓚ	36 Ⓕ Ⓖ Ⓗ Ⓙ Ⓚ
7 Ⓐ Ⓑ Ⓒ Ⓓ Ⓔ	17 Ⓐ Ⓑ Ⓒ Ⓓ Ⓔ	27 Ⓐ Ⓑ Ⓒ Ⓓ Ⓔ	37 Ⓐ Ⓑ Ⓒ Ⓓ Ⓔ
8 Ⓕ Ⓖ Ⓗ Ⓙ Ⓚ	18 Ⓕ Ⓖ Ⓗ Ⓙ Ⓚ	28 Ⓕ Ⓖ Ⓗ Ⓙ Ⓚ	38 Ⓕ Ⓖ Ⓗ Ⓙ Ⓚ
9 Ⓐ Ⓑ Ⓒ Ⓓ Ⓔ	19 Ⓐ Ⓑ Ⓒ Ⓓ Ⓔ	29 Ⓐ Ⓑ Ⓒ Ⓓ Ⓔ	39 Ⓐ Ⓑ Ⓒ Ⓓ Ⓔ
10 Ⓕ Ⓖ Ⓗ Ⓙ Ⓚ	20 Ⓕ Ⓖ Ⓗ Ⓙ Ⓚ	30 Ⓕ Ⓖ Ⓗ Ⓙ Ⓚ	40 Ⓕ Ⓖ Ⓗ Ⓙ Ⓚ

Scholastic Inc.

Scholastic Success With Math Tests • Grade 3   61

Practice Test 1 Tested Skills	Item Numbers
Numeration and Number Concepts	
Count by 2s, 10s	1, 2
Associate numerals and number words	3, 4
Compare and order whole numbers	6, 7
Use place value and rounding	8, 9, 10
Identify patterns	11, 12
Identify odd/even numbers	5, 13
Use number lines	14, 16
Estimation	15, 17
Identify fractional parts	19, 20
Compare and order fractions	24, 25
Use number sentences and operational properties	18, 21, 22, 23

Practice Test 2 Tested Skills	Item Numbers
Geometry and Measurement	
Identify plane and solid figures and their parts	6, 7, 8
Recognize symmetry and congruence	9, 10
Find area	11
Recognize value of money	3, 12
Tell time	2, 13
Use appropriate units of measurement	1, 16
Use measurement instruments	17, 18
Estimate measurements	14, 15
Identify transformations	19
Find coordinates on a grid	20
Interpret graphs, tables, charts	4, 5, 21, 22

Practice Test 3 Tested Skills	Item Numbers
Problem Solving	
Solve problems involving addition or subtraction	1–5
Solve problems involving multiplication or division	6–8
Solve problems involving money and time	9–12
Use estimation to solve problems	13–15
Solve problems involving probability or logic	16–18
Identify steps to solve a problem	19–21
Solve multi-step problems	22–24

Practice Test 4 Tested Skills	Item Numbers
Computation	
Add and subtract whole numbers	1–6
Multiply whole numbers	7–9
Divide whole numbers	12, 13
Add and subtract fractions	14, 17
Add and subtract decimals	18, 19, 20, 21
Find average, probability, and combinations	10, 11, 15, 16
Solve simple equations	22, 23, 24
Find coordinates on a grid	25, 26

Practice Test 5   Tested Skills

	Item Numbers
Numeration and Number Concepts	
Count by 2s, 10s	1, 2
Associate numerals and number words	3, 4
Compare and order whole numbers	6, 7
Use place value and rounding	8, 9, 10
Identify patterns	11, 12
Identify odd/even numbers	5, 13
Use number lines	14, 16
Estimation	15, 17
Identify fractional parts	19, 20
Compare and order fractions	24, 25
Use number sentences and operational properties	18, 21, 22, 23

Practice Test 6   Tested Skills

	Item Numbers
Geometry and Measurement	
Identify plane and solid figures and their parts	1, 3
Recognize symmetry and congruence	2, 4
Find area	5, 8
Recognize value of money	6, 7
Tell time	9, 10
Use appropriate units of measurement	11, 12
Use measurement instruments	13, 14, 15
Estimate measurements	16
Identify transformations	18
Find coordinates on a grid	17
Interpret graphs, tables, charts	19, 20, 21, 22

Practice Test 7   Tested Skills

	Item Numbers
Problem Solving	
Solve problems involving addition or subtraction	1–5
Solve problems involving multiplication or division	6–8
Solve problems involving money and time	9–12
Use estimation to solve problems	13–15
Solve problems involving probability or logic	16–18
Identify steps to solve a problem	19–21
Solve multi-step problems	22–24

Practice Test 8   Tested Skills

	Item Numbers
Computation	
Add and subtract whole numbers	1–6
Multiply whole numbers	7–9
Divide whole numbers	12, 13
Add and subtract fractions	14, 17, 18
Add and subtract decimals	19, 20, 21
Find average, probability, and combinations	10, 11, 15, 16
Solve simple equations	22, 23, 24
Find coordinates on a grid	25, 26

ANSWER KEY

Practice Test 1

Numeration and Number Concepts

1. B	14. G
2. J	15. C
3. D	16. H
4. H	17. B
5. A	18. J
6. G	19. D
7. D	20. F
8. G	21. C
9. B	22. G
10. H	23. A
11. A	24. J
12. H	25. B
13. D	

Practice Test 2

Geometry and Measurement

1. C	12. H
2. G	13. B
3. A	14. G
4. J	15. A
5. B	16. J
6. F	17. B
7. D	18. F
8. H	19. D
9. B	20. H
10. G	21. C
11. A	22. J

Practice Test 3

Problem Solving

1. B	13. B
2. J	14. G
3. A	15. C
4. H	16. F
5. E	17. D
6. H	18. J
7. B	19. A
8. F	20. H
9. D	21. B
10. K	22. G
11. C	23. E
12. K	24. J

Practice Test 4

Computation

1. D	14. H
2. G	15. B
3. B	16. F
4. J	17. A
5. E	18. G
6. H	19. C
7. C	20. J
8. K	21. D
9. A	22. H
10. G	23. A
11. D	24. G
12. J	25. B
13. E	26. J

Practice Test 5

Numeration and Number Concepts

1. B	14. G
2. H	15. A
3. C	16. J
4. F	17. B
5. D	18. F
6. J	19. D
7. D	20. G
8. G	21. A
9. C	22. J
10. G	23. B
11. A	24. F
12. H	25. D
13. C	

Practice Test 6

Geometry and Measurement

1. D	12. F
2. F	13. B
3. A	14. H
4. G	15. D
5. B	16. J
6. J	17. C
7. C	18. F
8. G	19. C
9. A	20. F
10. J	21. D
11. C	22. G

Practice Test 7

Problem Solving

1. B	13. C
2. H	14. J
3. E	15. B
4. G	16. F
5. C	17. A
6. J	18. H
7. B	19. E
8. K	20. G
9. E	21. D
10. H	22. F
11. D	23. C
12. K	24. H

Practice Test 8

Computation

1. C	14. K
2. K	15. B
3. B	16. F
4. J	17. A
5. B	18. J
6. H	19. E
7. D	20. H
8. F	21. A
9. A	22. J
10. G	23. C
11. A	24. G
12. G	25. A
13. D	26. H